Bibliographic information published by the German National Library:

The German National Library lists this publication in the National Bibliography; detailed bibliographic data are available on the Internet at http://dnb.dnb.de .

Imprint:

Copyright © 2017 GRIN Verlag
Print and binding: Books on Demand GmbH, Norderstedt Germany
ISBN: 9783668688834

This book at GRIN:

https://www.grin.com/document/421400

Anthony Kithome

Managing Threats of Cyber-Attacks on Mobile Devices

GRIN Verlag

Managing Threats of Cyber-Attacks on Mobile Devices

Contents

Abstract

Evidently, mobile phones and other mobile devices have taken over personal computers. They have become part of personal and business lives amongst the users. Regardless of they have brought unlimited challenges especially on issues of security. Cyber-attacks not only within individuals but also for businesses and government entities have threatened the welfare of mobile phones. Attacks on smartphones are on the high increase and quite sophisticated. This is quite alarming considering the fact that these devices are increasingly used to access and store sensitive personal information. In addition, they have also been used to conduct vital transactions such as in banking and online shopping. Vulnerability of attacks is high especially when attackers target unsuspecting users. Inasmuch as attacks target individuals, companies have also experienced similar threats that in the long run lead to massive losses whether as a result of breach of privacy and the risk of data loss or the resources used to secure the platforms. As a matter of fact, it has been estimated that cyber-attacks in mobile devices is very high as compared to personal computers. Nevertheless, the trend has been severed by ignorance of users who either fail to enable the security settings in their mobile devices or lack the resources to acquire more advanced mobile security. In overall, the industry has experienced laxity in providing up-to-date security technologies to secure mobile devices accordingly.

2

Managing Threats of Cyber-Attacks on Mobile Devices

Introduction

It is common knowledge that mobile devices have become important components of both business and personal lives. What started as the next generation of mobile phones have transformed into a mobile computer with combined capabilities of personal computers with hand held and mobile use (Shaulov, 2016). These devices have enough power to perform most of the functions of the PCs and have thus been targeted for cyber attacks by cyber criminals. According to Sheinis and Parker (2015), threats to mobile security has been on the rise as most mobile devices now have the capability of launching a distributed denial-of-service attack (DDoS attack) on the go. Equipped with large capacity storage, GBs of RAM and multiprocessor, most mobile devices can easily be used for DDoS attacks. Besides, these voices are increasingly vulnerable from SideSteppers and DroidJack which can be found in third-party stores. At the same time, they are also vulnerable to remote access from cyber criminals. This research paper adopted a qualitative approach based on the evaluation of past studies that has been conducted on the topic. In order to make valid conclusions, I will conduct a content analysis of several study reports. Using the content analysis procedure, the paper will attempt to answer the following research questions: What are the potential cyber-attack threats on mobile devices?; How safe are the mobile devices when used for personal or business purposes?; How to manage threats of cyber-attacks on mobile device?

Literature review

Based on studies, it has proved that over 90% of mobile users keep their devices within an arm's reach most of the time (Wright, Dawson & Omar, 2012). In that regard, it can be ascertained that the mobile devices have largely revolutionized the contemporary life. They are increasingly used for both personal and business requirements. Smartphones or simply mobile phones with advanced capabilities similar to those of personal computers (PCs) are increasingly filling people's pockets, purses and even briefcases. This has however been without its challenges. The increasing popularity of the smartphones has brought unrelenting harms in the industry. This is particularly the case especially considering security laxity in the area. Mobiles phones and more so advanced gadgets as in the case of smartphones have been considered as attractive targets for attacks. Based on studies, attacks on mobile devices and the accompanying Apps are overly on the rise (**Yesilyurt & Yalman, 2016**). This has generally been hampered by the fact that enterprises technically fall short in protecting corporate data within mobile apps and devices. It is estimated that a small fraction of companies (around 8%) enforces OS updates with less 5% applying App Reputation or Mobile Threat Detection software (**Yesilyurt & Yalman, 2016**).

Currently, smartphones have almost outsold PCs. It is in this view that attackers have taken advantage of the expanding market. To accomplish their malice practices, they use both old techniques and emerging ones to cause havoc in the industry. A typical example of serious mobile phones attack, the Valentine's Day attack happened in year 2011 (**Yeboah-Boateng & Amanor, 2014**). In the attack, attackers succeeded in distributing a mobile picture-sharing application that in the process secretly sent premium-rate text messages from user's mobile phones. In one study, from 2009 to 2010, the rate of vulnerabilities in the mobile operating systems increased tremendously. Inasmuch as the rate and sophistication of such attacks on mobiles escalates, countermeasures seem quite slow and incapable of catching up with the menace (**Yeboah-Boateng & Amanor, 2014**).

4

Typically, smartphones as well as personal digital assistants (PDAs) provide users with mobile opportunity to access their emails, internet, and GPS navigation alongside other major applications. Regardless of the increasing usage of mobile devices, smartphone security has failed to maintain the standards of traditional computer security. Such technical security measures like firewalls, antivirus and encryption are rare in mobile phones. Besides, mobile phone operating systems are never updated often as compared to those of personal computers (Wright, Dawson & Omar, 2012). In some instances, applications for social networking within mobile phones do not have detailed privacy controls in relation to the PC counterparts. It has however been noted that majority of smartphone users completely disregard the security inadequacies in their devices. This provides attack with the opportunity to unleash their terror to the unsuspecting users. Though in most cases the smartphones come with already installed security software, ignorant users fail to enable and activate it. Majority surf the internet in the belief that their phones are less vulnerable as compared to the PCs. In the real sense, mobile phones accomplish many tasks and as well store sensitive data, for instance, emails, contact information and passwords (Wright, Dawson & Omar, 2012). This is quite the case especially in the view of how the devices are used for social networking purposes which typically maintain high volumes of personal information. Emerging innovations in the field of mobile commerce has made possible for users to carryout financial transactions like purchasing of goods as well as vast applications over wireless networks. Other includes redeeming of coupons and tickets, processing point-of-sale payments, banking and even in paying in cash registers.

Potential cyber-attack threats on mobile devices

Although it has been said that mobile devices, like computers, pose a great threat to security in various parts of the world, the truth is that it is the people, and not the mobile devices,

5

that is creating the threats. In most cases, it is humans using computers to victimize other mobile devices and mobile device users for their own good. Given space on the internet, computer hackers will increase the security threats exponentially. While there might be many definitions of hacking, hackers are generally considered to be individuals who use unauthorized means to break into computers and computer systems in order to destroy, change or steal information (Shaulov, 2016). In order to achieve their purposes, hackers will often install dangerous malware without the consent or knowledge of the mobile devices users. In order to achieve their objectives, hackers must be clever in their detail and tactics and must have excellent computer knowledge in order to access the information they want. Irrespective of the definition, hacking is considered to be a crime in many parts of the world. Hackers expose unsuspecting individuals to loss of personal information and economic inconvenience while also making it hard for the law enforcement agency to arrest and prosecute cyber criminals.

While most mobile devices users feel that they might be free from hackers, the reality is that any mobile devices users can be victims of hackers. Although the majority of hacking occurs online, where computer networks are used to facilitate the crime, even offline computer users are not safe. Indeed, most of the hacking takes place offline when the hackers use software to gain access to mobile devices and computer systems to gain access to various types of information, including the logging details and other personal information about the users (Shaulov, 2016). Once this personal information is acquired, the owner of such information is left at the mercy of the hackers. In most cases, the stolen information is used for the purposes of identity theft. Similarly, for individuals working online, the threat of hacking is still there. The internet is filled with individuals seeking to take advantage of unsuspecting internet users to enrich themselves. This is often done by using Wi-fi, Bluetooth or infrared the to gain access to the mobile devices belonging to individuals to get personal information such as bank details, credit card numbers, email passwords and much other personal information that can facilitate them to defraud their victims. Basically, hackers are close to many people more than they can imagine.

Just like mobile devices, mobile viruses have come of age. The level of sophistication of modern mobile viruses has perplexed many people. During the inception of computing, the development of computers was mainly used fun and a means of causing annoyance. In recent times, however, designers of computer viruses and malware have turned into professionals developing sophisticated malware that has threatened global computing. Over the recent past, new viruses have emerged that have changed the course of mobile computing. Mobile virus and malware are mainly aimed at obtaining information from without the consent of the owners of such information. This means malware developers obtain information without the consent of the owners. The majority of information obtained in this way is aimed at causing harm. In most cases, developers use their knowledge to access mobiles and computer systems without the consent of the owners of the computers. The lack of consent from owners of such computers and computer systems is what makes malware and virus illegal (Shaulov, 2016). While many mobile virus developers have claimed that there is an art and obsession that leaders to innovation, the majority of the people still believe that most virus developers are motivated by the desire to harm rather than the desire to fight for the common good of the people.

How safe are the mobile devices when used for personal or business purposes?

While the levels of risks for mobile devices when used for personal purposes is not as high as the risk faced by mobile devices in offices and organizations, personal use cannot be ignored when it comes to mobile security concerns. The reduced level of risk for personal use does not mean that they are safe. The cost of lost identity or data is substantial enough to justify considerations. With regards to mobile devices, personal use is no different from organizational usage save for the fact that under personal usage, the device is less likely to be connected to an organizational network (Sheinis & Parker, 2015). Nevertheless, the fact that mobile devices are used for storing personal information, important data, among other things means that they require substantial security considerations.

The most common risk for mobile devices, under personal and organizational use, is a computer virus. Trojan, horses, and worms are some of the most common threats to mobile devices. This virus can be acquired through the internet or communicated through infected flash drives. Like business mobile devices, personal mobile devices will often malefactions when infected with viruses. This means the user of the device will face inconveniences relating to the devices slowing down or damages to files. Besides, mobile devices infected with viruses will often experience system crashes and reduced productivity (Borrett, Carter & Wespi, 2013).To prevent infections from viruses, mobile devices, for personal or business use, must be protected with anti-viruses. Besides, the anti-virus definition must be updated frequently.

Mobile devices, both for business and personal usage, are likely to be targeted for identity theft. Because mobile devices are frequently used to access the internet, it is possible that the identity of the owner is stolen and used for unscrupulous purposes. One of the major fears of using the internet on mobile devices, therefore, is the possibility of identity theft. This is where personal and confidential information is used by cyber criminals to carry out criminal activities (Shaulov, 2016). There are various ways through which this can be achieved. The most used means of accessing personal identity is the use of malware. In the year 2012, for example, a virus named Flame rose to fame by specifically targeting home computers. This virus was spread through USB disks or through Local Area Networks (Stiakakis, Georgiadis, & Andronoudi,

8

2016). Unlike most viruses, this virus was able to acquire information by recording audio information, acquire and send screenshots and monitor the network traffic (Borrett, Carter & Wespi, 2013). It was also able to record conversations over Skype and monitor keyboard activities. Given the realization that this virus had Microsoft certificates, it was regarded by most anti-viruses as being authentic and thus hard to discover. Such kinds of threats are as true for mobile devices just as they are for computers.

Other major security risks on mobile devices might include unintentional data loss, accidental deletion of files and deletion of applications or application files. The problem of accidental data and program loss on mobile devices is increased by the fact that most mobile devices are personal and most owners log in as administrators (Borrett, Carter & Wespi, 2013). As administrators, the device allows the owners to make changes to the device, including deleting programs without being asked for a password. When these deletions occur accidentally, important data might be lost. Such kinds of problems might not be apparent when the mobile devices are used in the business setting because the users are not the administrators are will most likely be required to input passwords before any deletions.

How to manage threats of cyber-attacks on mobile device

There are various ways in which cyber threats on mobile devices can be managed. Most mobile device manufacturers were well aware of the possible cyber attacks on the devices and have implemented various ways that can be used by the device owners to manage cyber threats. One of the features that mobile phone manufacturers have used is the provisions of cloud storage services for the phones users. Android, users have about 15GBs of free cloud storage. Users can use the cloud to store the sensitive data and encrypt them is they feel the need to do so. The most impressive aspects cloud storage is the fact that mobile device owners can remotely delete their

9

data when they have lost their devices or when they feel that their personal data is under some threat(Borrett, Carter & Wespi, 2013). The remote functionality makes it possible for individuals to protect their data even when they have lost the control of the devices. Besides, most modern mobile devices give the owners the options of remotely deleting their applications, confidential data stored in the device and contacts. Such capabilities are put into place to ensure that individual's data are not easily stolen even when their devices have been stolen.

Far from the security management options put into place by the manufacturers, there are various management options that individuals can use to protect themselves from data attacks. For mobile device users, the most effective cyber attack management options are to disable unnecessary or unused mobile features such as Bluetooth, Wi-fi or infrared. These connectivity features can easily be used by data thieves and hackers to gain access to the device and access vital information (Stiakakis, Georgiadis, & Andronoudi, 2016). In particular, individuals should ensure that they disable their connectivity options when they are in public places or when they are in company strangers. Besides, it is important to scrutinize and only use free wi-fi when the risks have been calculated or when the source of the wi-fi is known. Similarly, it is important to enable the firewall and disable the sharing options whenever in public places. the aim is to ensure that all the available options for remote connectivity are disabled so that unintended or malicious connections are made imposable.

Far from the external threats, there are the internal threats that the device owner must also manage. From the outset, it is important to separate corporate apps from personal apps. Confusing or mismanaging any of the two categories of apps can result into security vulnerability and can lead to data loss (Stiakakis, Georgiadis, & Andronoudi, 2016). Further, there is need to install anti-virus programs on the mobile devices. Although anti-virus has traditionally been used on desktop computers, there are many anti-virus apps for mobile devices that can be used to prevent the threats of virus and malware. Most importantly, given that most cyber threats effective mobile devices come from the internet, it is important that mobile devices users be conscious of the sites they are visiting and downloading their materials. In particular, the mobile device owners must ensure that the apps they install on their devices are obtained from trusted applications provides. Nonetheless, given that not many people are able to differentiations trusted applications providers from the entrusted ones, it is important to take a cue from the permission request by the device during installation (Borrett, Carter & Wespi, 2013).

Conclusion

In sum, access to the internet remains the main security risks for mobile devices. Accessing the internet exposes a mobile device to virtually all the risks discussed above. Unsecured internet access, particularly through wi-fi increases the risk of hackers gaining access to a mobile device. Given the realization that the internet has become part and parcel of modern computing, it is impossible that a mobile device will work without period access to the internet. In this regard, it is incumbent upon home computers owners to put into place sufficient security measures, such as installing anti-viruses, to protect themselves against cyber criminals and other Internet-related security threats. Besides, backing up files might be a better way of remaining safe from security threats. By backing up files, an individual is assured of his data even when the computer has been affected by a virus or accidental data deletion. Most importantly, the use of cloud computing can come in handy for remote management of personal data stored on the mobile devices.

References

Borrett, M., Carter, R., & Wespi, A. (2013). How is cyber threat evolving and what do organizations need to consider? *Journal of Business Continuity & Emergency Planning*, *7*(2), 163-171.

Flinders, K. (2015). Mobile Security -- What Works And What Doesn't. *Computer Weekly*, 25-28.

Shaulov, M. (2016). Bridging mobile security gaps. *Network Security*, *2016*(1), 5-8.

Sheinis, R., & Parker, F. (2015). Hacking The Cyber Threat Landscape for 2015. (Cover story). *Hospitality Upgrade*, 12-24.

Stiakakis, E., Georgiadis, C., & Andronoudi, A. (2016). Users' perceptions about mobile security breaches. *Information Systems & E-Business Management*, *14*(4), 857-882

Wright, J., Dawson, M. & Omar, M., (2012). Cyber Security and Mobile Threats: The Need for Antivirus Applications for Smart Phones. *Journal of Information Systems Technology & Planning*, 5(14), 40-60.

Yesilyurt, M. & Yalman, Y., (2016). Security Threats on Mobile Devices and their Effects: Estimations for the Future. *International Journal of Security and Its Applications*, 10(2): 13-26.

Yeboah-Boateng, E. & Amanor, P., (2014). Phishing, SMiShing & Vishing: An Assessment of Threats against Mobile Devices. Journal of Emerging Trends in Computing and Information Sciences, 5(4): 297-305.